TALAWA THEATRE COMPANY AND THE ROYAL _ _ _

Superhoe

by Nicôle Lecky

Superhoe was presented at Talawa Firsts in June 2018.

Superhoe was first performed at the Royal Court Jerwood
Theatre Upstairs, Sloane Square, on Wednesday 30 January 2019.

Superhoe
by Nicôle Lecky

CAST

Sasha Clayton **Nicôle Lecky**

Director **Jade Lewis**
Design Consultant **Chloe Lamford**
Costume Designer **Kiera Liberati**
Lighting Designer **Prema Mehta**
Music **The Last Skeptik & Nicôle Lecky**
Sound Designer **Emma Laxton**
Graphics & Video Designer **Ewan Jones Morris**
Movement Director **Sara Dos Santos**
Dialect Coach **Hazel Holder**
Costume Supervisor **Lucy Walshaw**
Production Manager **Marty Moore**
Stage Managers **Nic Donithorn, Olivia Roberts**
Set built by **Royal Court Stage Department**

Talawa Theatre Company, The Royal Court & Stage Management wish to thank the following
for their help with this production:
Kiell Smith-Bynoe & Matt Wills for contribution to music.

Superhoe
by Nicôle Lecky

Nicôle Lecky (Writer/Performer)

As performer, theatre includes: **The Tenant of Wildfell Hall/The Railway Children (Octagon, Bolton); This Heaven (Finborough).**

As performer, television includes: **SENSE8, Death in Paradise, Doctors, Casualty, Silent Witness, Edge of Heaven, Fresh Meat.**

Nicôle is an English-Jamaican writer and actress from the East End. She was part of Soho Theatre's Writers Lab 2016–2017 and is a recent recipient of the Creative Skillset & Dancing Ledge Productions' High-end Television Levy Writers' Bursary. Nicôle story-lined for Series 3 of *Ackley Bridge* and wrote *Student Body* for The Almeida for their participation programme. She also wrote for series 1 & 2 of *Eastenders: E20*, as well as story-lining at Big Talk for the E4 series *Youngers*.

Sara Dos Santos
(Movement Director)

Theatre includes: **Astro Babies (Ovalhouse); Rainman (The Place); Miles Ahead (Cochrane); Four Walls (Peepul Center, Leicester).**

As choreographer, theatre includes: **Frontline (The Place); Journey's (Trinity Centre, Bristol); Redemption (Trinity Laban); Missing Her (Centro Cultural UGF, Brazil); Traded (Swan, Wycombe).**

Awards include: **British Council IETM Porto Bursary Award; Neriah Kumah Legacy Gift supported by One Dance UK; One Dance UK - Dancers Mentoring Programme Award.**

Sara is a London based movement artist, choreographer and movement director, working across multiple disciplines of theatre, performance installations and film. She runs a variation of movement and dance workshops for institutions and community groups across the UK. Sara was Artistic Director of Curve Creative Dance Company 2017–18 and of East London Youth Dance Company 2015–17.

Ewan Jones Morris
(Graphics & Video Designer)

Ewan is a filmmaker, director and animator who takes a multidisciplinary approach to filmmaking, combining live action, collage, stop motion and CGI to transform the ordinary and explore imagined inner worlds. His music video work has attracted a number of awards, having directed and co-directed videos for the likes of John Grant, Leftfield, DJ Shadow, The Human League, Cate Le Bon and Anna Meredith. Ewan has collaborated with artist Bedwyr Williams on a number of films including *Starry Messenger*, *Echt*, *Century Egg* and most recently *Flexure* which screened as part of Williams' Barbican exhibition in The Curve.

Ewan collaborated with comedian Daniel Kitson, creating films of his theatre pieces *It's Always Right Now Until It's Later* and *Tree*, and his work is regularly featured at Adam Buxton's BFI fixture *BUG*. Ewan's recent BFI funded short film *This Far Up* won a Bafta Cymru award for best short in 2017.

His most recent collaboration was on *TBCTV*, a performance and moving image exhibition for Somerset House Studios with Mel Brimfield and Royal Court Associate Designer Chloe Lamford.

Chloe Lamford (Design Consultant)

For the Royal Court: **The Cane, Pity, Gundog, My Mum's a Twat, Grimly Handsome [co-creator], The Site Programme, Victory Condition, B, Road, Nuclear War, Unreachable, Ophelia's Zimmer (& Schaubühne, Berlin), How to Hold Your Breath, God Bless the Child, 2071, Teh Internet Is Serious Business, Open Court 2013, Circle Mirror Transformation.**

Other theatre includes: **The Crucible (Theater Basel); TBCTV (Somerset House); Hamilton Complex (Schauspielhaus, Bochum); John, Amadeus, Rules for Living, The World of Extreme Happiness (National); 1984 (Headlong/Almeida/West End/Broadway); The Maids (Toneelgroep, Amsterdam); The Tempest, Salt Root & Roe (Donmar); Shakespeare's Last Play, Atmen (Schaubühne, Berlin); Our Ladies of Perpetual Succour (& Live/National/West End/International tour), My Shrinking Life, An Appointment with the Wicker Man, Knives In Hens (National Theatre of Scotland); Britney & Goofy, Het Hamiltoncomplex (Hetpaleis, Antwerp); The Events (ATC/Young Vic); Disco Pigs, Sus, Blackta [costume] (Young Vic); Praxis Makes Perfect, The Radicalisation of Bradley Manning (National Theatre Wales); Boys (Headlong/Soho); Jubilee, Cannibals, The Gate Keeper (Royal Exchange, Manchester); My Romantic History (& Bush), The History Boys (Crucible, Sheffield); Joseph K, The Kreutzer Sonata (Gate); it felt empty... (Clean Break/Arcola); Everything Must Go!, This Wide Night (Soho); The Mother Ship, How to Tell the Monsters from the Misfits (Birmingham Rep); Small Miracle (Kiln/Mercury, Colchester).**

Opera & dance includes: **Verklärte Nacht (Rambert, Chor: Kim Brandstrup); Miranda (Opera Comique, Paris); Ariadne Auf Naxos, Alcina, Pelleas & Melisande (Aix-en-Provence Festival); The Little Sweep, Let's Make an Opera (Malmo Opera House, Sweden); The Magic Flute (English Touring Opera); War & Peace (Scottish Opera/RCS).**

Awards include: **Arts Foundation Fellowship Award for Design for Performance in Set & Costume, Theatrical Management Association Award for Best Theatre Design (Small Miracle).**

The Last Skeptik (Music)

Corin Douieb AKA The Last Skeptik is a DJ, producer and composer who has toured the world and scored music for television, commercials, film and theatre. His solo debut album *Thanks For Trying* **was released on BBE Records and was a genre-defying journey through hip-hop and electronic music. This was followed by** *This Is Where It Gets Good* **in 2017 – supported by Complex, BBC Radio 1, 1Xtra and The Quietus, the album featured an orchestra of musicians and navigated a dark, twisted journey through surviving in London, battling with mental health problems and coming out the other side.**

Skeptik's latest release, *Under the Patio,* **features artists such as Kojey Radical, The Manor and Doc Brown, and was featured heavily on Apple Music and Spotify's curated playlists. Recent years have seen Skeptik produce for some of the UK's best and most diverse artists (including the likes of Giggs and Mikill Pane), have guest mixes featured on Vice, I–D, DefJam.com, BBC Radio 1 and 1Xtra, as well as compose the soundtrack to a BAFTA nominated short film,** *Island Queen.*

As a touring DJ, Skeptik has performed around the globe at events such as Coachella and SXSW, toured India, Japan and the Middle East, supported Charli XCX on her US tour and opened for the likes of 2Chainz, Damon Albarn, The Libertines, Childish Gambino and Wu Tang Clan. His Forbes Magazine recommended podcast *Thanks For Trying* **has sold out theatres and is regularly on the front page of iTunes, hosting special guests such as Taika Waititi, Katherine Ryan, Romesh Ranganathan, Sara Pascoe, Kurupt FM & Ed Skrein among many others.**

Emma Laxton (Sound Designer)

For the Royal Court: **Rita, Sue & Bob Too (& Out of Joint).**

Other theatre includes: **Uncle Vanya (Hampstead); Measure for Measure, The York Realist, The Lady from the Sea, Limehouse (Donmar); Sweet Charity (Nottingham Playhouse); Elizabeth (Barbican); The Writer (Almeida); The Country Wife, random/generations, The Chalk Garden, The House They Grew Up In, Forty Years On (Chichester Festival); Titus Andronicus (RSC/ Barbican); Julius Caesar, The Effect (Crucible, Sheffield); See Me Now (Young Vic); Breaking the Code, All My Sons, A Doll's House, Three Birds, The Accrington Pals (Royal Exchange, Manchester); Ghosts, The Orestela (HOME, Manchester); Made in Dagenham (Queen's, Hornchurch/New Wolsey, Ipswich).**

Awards include: **Falstaff Award for Best Sound Design/Original Score (Coriolanus).**

Emma was previously Deputy Head of Sound for the Royal Court, the Associate Sound Designer for the National Theatre's production of *War Horse* **and an Associate Artist at the Bush Theatre.**

Jade Lewis (Director)

As assistant director, for the Royal Court: **a profoundly affectionate, passionate devotion to someone (-noun).**

As writer/director, theatre includes: **Astro Babies (Ovalhouse).**

As director, theatre includes: **Extinguished Things (Summerhall/Adelaide Fringe); Quarter Life Crisis (Underbelly/Soho); On the Edge of Me (Soho/Rich Mix).**

As movement director, theatre includes: **Followers (Southwark).**

As assistant director, other theatre includes: **Nine Night (National/Trafalgar Studios); The Convert, Iphigenia Quartet (Gate); Madness Sweet Madness (Martin Harris, Manchester/Lantern, Liverpool); Venus/Mars (Old Red Lion/Bush).**

Jade was a Boris Karloff Trainee Assistant Director at the Young Vic. She was a Creative Associate at The Gate Theatre and one of Ovalhouse's Emerging Artist team. She has also directed and assisted on community projects for Southwark Playhouse, Southbank Centre, Company 3 and The Young Vic.

Kiera Liberati (Costume Designer)

Kiera is a forward thinking fashion/celebrity stylist and consultant based in London. Working across all aspects of styling and creative consulting, her work covers editorial, music videos, press and marketing material, campaigns and branding, art direction and editing.

Kiera has styled artists including Zara Larsson, Wretch 32, The Manor, Julie Adenuga, Niall Horan, Mic Lowry, Liam Gallagher, Future, WSTRN and Tink for various campaigns, television and live events, including The Jonathan Ross Show, BBC Live Lounge and Push magazine. She has also styled music videos for artists such as J Hus, Little Mix, Big Shaq, Geko, Alex Hepburn and Nick Brewer.

Kiera's commercial work includes campaigns for Reebok, K-Swiss, Adidas, Lynx, Nike and USA Pro. She is currently the Fashion Director for Notion Magazine.

Prema Mehta (Lighting Designer)

Theatre includes: Things of Dry Hours (Young Vic); East Is East (& Northern Stage), Hercules, Holes (Nottingham Playhouse); A Passage to India (Royal & Derngate, Northampton/UK tour); Mighty Atoms (Hull Truck); Everything is Possible: The York Suffragettes, Murder Margaret & Me (Theatre Royal, York); Talking Heads (Leeds Playhouse); Love, Lies & Taxidermy, Growth, I Got Superpowers for My Birthday (Paines Plough); Coming Up, Jefferson's Garden, Fourteen (Watford Palace); Wipers, Made in India (UK tour); Lady Anna: All at Sea (Theatre Royal, Bath/UK tour); Red Snapper (Belgrade, Coventry); The Electric Hills (Liverpool Everyman); The Great Extension (Theatre Royal Stratford East); The Snow Queen (Derby Theatre); Jack & the Beanstalk, Beauty & the Beast (Queen's, Hornchurch); Huddle (Unicorn); Of Kith & Kin (& Bush), Chicken Soup (Crucible, Sheffield); Fame (Selladoor/UK tour); The Wizard of Oz (Storyhouse); A Midsummer Night's Dream (Curve, Leicester); With a Little Bit of Luck (Latitude Festival); Spring Awakening (National Youth Music Theatre).

Dance includes: Bells (Mayor of London Presents: Showtime Festival); The Puppini Sisters (Bloomsbury); Penguin Café (Cochrane/London College of Fashion); Spill (Düsseldorf); Sufi Zen (Royal Festival Hall); Dhamaka (O2 Arena); Maaya (Westminster Hall).

Talawa Theatre Company

'… an impassioned performance … its emotional punch feels very real.'
**** *Evening Standard (Half Breed)*

'… terrific from the get-go with huge style and verve.'
**** *The Times (Guys & Dolls)*

Talawa is one of the most successful Black theatre companies in the UK. We have established a track record of producing work which shines a spotlight on Black artists, creating theatre for diverse audiences across the country. Mounting more than fifty productions over our 32-year history, recent productions have included the hugely successful collaborations with the Royal Exchange Theatre including; *Guys & Dolls*, music and lyrics by Frank Loesser, book by Jo Swerling and Abe Burrows (Royal Exchange Theatre and Talawa Theatre Company co-production), *King Lear* by William Shakespeare (in association with Birmingham Repertory Theatre) and *All My Sons* by Arthur Miller (Royal Exchange Theatre, UK tour).

Talawa's ongoing artist development activity has enabled the company to identify, nurture and champion some of the most exciting Black playwrights and theatre makers in the UK today, some of whom have had their work co-produced with us, including *Girls* by Theresa Ikoko (co-production with Soho Theatre, HighTide) and *Half Breed* by Natasha Marshall (co-production with Soho Theatre).

'Theatre is vital to our lives, it's important to see oneself reflected in the arts, and at Talawa this is our aim.'

Michael Buffong, Artistic Director, Talawa Theatre Company

Talawa was founded in 1986 by Black artists and activists Yvonne Brewster OBE, Mona Hammond, Carmen Munroe and Inigo Espejel, in order to address the lack of opportunities for Black actors on British stages. The vision was to diversify the theatre industry; making it fully representative of the UK's population. Today, led by Artistic Director Michael Buffong, Talawa dedicates its resources to creating high quality touring productions and to developing Black artists. The company enables this by:

• Producing one national touring production a year.
• Developing a canon of new Black British plays through commissioning, training and giving dramaturgical feedback through the free to use bi-annual script reading service.
• Supporting the careers of over 250 Black theatre artists, backstage staff and administrators annually by offering training, mentoring, and a chance to develop and present creative ideas through our artistic development programme MAKE.
• Using theatre as a learning and/or personal development tool in schools, community groups and in businesses.

The Talawa Team

Michael Buffong – Artistic Director
Natasha Bucknor – Executive Director
Sanjit Chudha – Marketing & Communications Manager
Anthony Lennon – Associate Director
Zewditu Bekele – Finance Manager
Rachel Barker – Project Manager
Pooja Sitpura - Producer, Participation & Learning
Jane Fallowfield - Literary Associate
Myah Jeffers - New Work Co-ordinator
Camara Pinnock - Development & Marketing Co-ordinator
Tricia Wey - Administrator

Talawa would like to thank everyone at the Royal Court for making this production possible.

Support

We are grateful for the support of Arts Council England, Esmée Fairbairn Foundation, John Ellerman Foundation, City Bridge Trust, The Martin Bowley Charitable Trust, The Orseis Trust, and BBC Writersroom.

Talawa is a registered charity (No.327362). Any money that we earn or raise is reinvested back into the work that we do. With your help we can continue to tour engaging and powerful theatre for audiences across the UK and support the next generation of Black artists.

Visit us at talawa.com/support-us to find out how you can help. Details of Talawa's new supporter's scheme will be announced in the Spring.

ARTS COUNCIL ENGLAND

THE ROYAL COURT THEATRE

The Royal Court Theatre is the writers' theatre. It is a leading force in world theatre for energetically cultivating writers – undiscovered, emerging and established.

Through the writers, the Royal Court is at the forefront of creating restless, alert, provocative theatre about now. We open our doors to the unheard voices and free thinkers that, through their writing, change our way of seeing.

Over 120,000 people visit the Royal Court in Sloane Square, London, each year and many thousands more see our work elsewhere through transfers to the West End and New York, UK and international tours, digital platforms, our residencies across London, and our site-specific work. Through all our work we strive to inspire audiences and influence future writers with radical thinking and provocative discussion.

The Royal Court's extensive development activity encompasses a diverse range of writers and artists and includes an ongoing programme of writers' attachments, readings, workshops and playwriting groups. Twenty years of the International Department's pioneering work around the world means the Royal Court has relationships with writers on every continent.

Within the past sixty years, John Osborne, Samuel Beckett, Arnold Wesker, Ann Jellicoe, Howard Brenton and David Hare have started their careers at the Court. Many others including Caryl Churchill, Athol Fugard, Mark Ravenhill, Simon Stephens, debbie tucker green, Sarah Kane – and, more recently, Lucy Kirkwood, Nick Payne, Penelope Skinner and Alistair McDowall – have followed.

The Royal Court has produced many iconic plays from Lucy Kirkwood's **The Children** to Jez Butterworth's **Jerusalem** and Martin McDonagh's **Hangmen**.

Royal Court plays from every decade are now performed on stage and taught in classrooms and universities across the globe.

It is because of this commitment to the writer that we believe there is no more important theatre in the world than the Royal Court.

Supported using public funding by
ARTS COUNCIL ENGLAND

COMING UP AT THE ROYAL COURT

14 Feb - 23 Mar

Cyprus Avenue

By David Ireland

Abbey Theatre and Royal Court Theatre.

27 Feb - 23 Mar

Inside Bitch

**Conceived by Stacey Gregg
& Deborah Pearson
Devised by Lucy Edkins,
Jennifer Joseph, TerriAnn Oudjar
and Jade Small**

Clean Break and Royal Court Theatre.

3 - 27 Apr

Pah–La

By Abhishek Majumdar

10 May - 15 Jun

White Pearl

By Anchuli Felicia King

14 May - 1 Jun

salt.

By Selina Thompson

Commissioned by MAYK, Theatre Bristol and Yorkshire Festival.

27 Jun - 10 Aug

the end of history...

By Jack Thorne

4 - 27 Jul

seven methods of killing kylie jenner

By Jasmine Lee–Jones

royalcourttheatre.com

Sloane Square London, SW1W 8AS ⊖ Sloane Square
⇌ Victoria Station 🐦 royalcourt 🇫 royalcourttheatre

Supported using public funding by
**ARTS COUNCIL
ENGLAND**

ASSISTED PERFORMANCES

Captioned Performances

Captioned performances are accessible for D/deaf, deafened & hard of hearing people as well as being suitable for people for whom English is not a first language.

In the Jerwood Theatre Downstairs
Cyprus Avenue: Tue 12 Mar, 7.30pm
White Pearl: Wed 22 & 29 May, 5 & 12 Jun, 7.30pm
the end of history...: Wed 10, 17 (plus live speech-to-text pos show talk), 24, 31 Jul & 7 Aug 7.30pm

In the Jerwood Theatre Upstairs
Inside Bitch: Wed 20 March, 7.45pm
Pah-La: Wed 24 April, 7.45pm
salt.: Fri 31 May, 7.45pm
seven methods of killing kylie jenner: Fri 19 & 26 Jul, 7.45

Audio Described Performances

Audio described performances are accessible for blind or partia sighted customers. They are preceded by a touch tour (at 1pm) which allows patrons access to elements of theatre design includ set & costume.

In the Jerwood Theatre Downstairs
Cyprus Avenue: Sat 9 March, 2.30pm
White Pearl: Sat 8 June, 2.30pm
the end of history...: Sat 3 Aug, 2.30pm

ROYAL

ASSISTED PERFORMANCES

Performances in a Relaxed Environment

Relaxed Environment performances are suitable for those who may benefit from a more relaxed experience.

During these performances:

- There will be a relaxed attitude to noise in the auditorium; you are welcome to respond to the show in whatever way feels natural
- You can enter and exit the auditorium when needed
- We will help you find the best seats
- House lights remained raised slightly

Inside Bitch: Sat 23 Mar, 3pm
salt.: Sat 25 May, 7.45pm
White Pearl: Sat 1 Jun, 2.30pm
The end of history...: Sat 27 Jul, 2.30pm

If you would like to talk to us about your access requirements please contact our Box Office at (0)20 7565 5000 or **boxoffice@royalcourttheatre.com.** A Royal Court Visual Story is available on our website. We also produce a Story Synopsis & Sensory Synopsis which are available on request.

For more information and to book access tickets online, visit

royalcourttheatre.com/assisted-performances

Sloane Square London, SW1W 8AS ⊖ Sloane Square ⇄ Victoria Station
royalcourt royalcourttheatre

COURT

ROYAL COURT SUPPORTERS

The Royal Court is a registered charity and not-for-profit company. We need to raise £1.5 million every year in addition to our core grant from the Arts Council and our ticket income to achieve what we do.

We have significant and longstanding relationships with many generous organisations and individuals who provide vital support. Royal Court supporters enable us to remain the writers' theatre, find stories from everywhere and create theatre for everyone.

We can't do it without you.

PUBLIC FUNDING

Arts Council England, London
British Council

TRUSTS & FOUNDATIONS

The Backstage Trust
The Bryan Adams Charitable Trust
The Austin & Hope Pilkington Trust
The Boshier-Hinton Foundation
Martin Bowley Charitable Trust
The Chapman Charitable Trust
Gerald Chapman Fund
CHK Charities
The City Bridge Trust
The Cleopatra Trust
The Clifford Chance Foundation
Cockayne - Grants for the Arts
The Ernest Cook Trust
The Nöel Coward Foundation
Cowley Charitable Trust
The Eranda Rothschild Foundation
Lady Antonia Fraser for The Pinter Commission
Genesis Foundation
The Golden Bottle Trust
The Haberdashers' Company
The Paul Hamlyn Foundation
Roderick & Elizabeth Jack
Jerwood Charitable Foundation
The Leche Trust
The Andrew Lloyd Webber Foundation
The London Community Foundation
John Lyon's Charity
Clare McIntyre's Bursary
Old Possum's Practical Trust
The Andrew W. Mellon Foundation
The David & Elaine Potter Foundation
The Richard Radcliffe Charitable Trust
Rose Foundation
Royal Victoria Hall Foundation
The Sackler Trust
The Sobell Foundation
Span Trust
John Thaw Foundation
Unity Theatre Trust
The Wellcome Trust
The Garfield Weston Foundation

CORPORATE SPONSORS

Aqua Financial Solutions Ltd
Cadogan Estates
Colbert
Edwardian Hotels, London
Fever-Tree
Gedye & Sons
Greene King
Kirkland & Ellis International LLP
Kudos
MAC
Room One
Sister Pictures

CORPORATE MEMBERS

Gold
Weil, Gotshal & Manges LLP

Silver
Auerbach & Steele Opticians
Bloomberg
Cream
Kekst CNC
Left Bank Pictures
Love My Human
PATRIZIA
Royal Bank of Canada - Global Asset Management
Tetragon Financial Group

For more information or to become a foundation or business supporter contact: support@royalcourttheatre.com/020 7565 5064.

INDIVIDUAL SUPPORTERS

Artistic Director's Circle
Eric Abraham
Carolyn Bennett
Samantha & Richard
  Campbell-Breeden
Cas Donald
Jane Featherstone
Lydia & Manfred Gorvy
Jean & David Grier
Charles Holloway
Luke Johnson
Jack & Linda Keenan
Mandeep & Sarah Manku
Anatol Orient
NoraLee & Jon Sedmak
Deborah Shaw
  & Stephen Marquardt
Matthew & Sian Westerman
Mahdi Yahya

Writers' Circle
Chris & Alison Cabot
Jordan Cook & John Burbank
Scott M. Delman
Virginia Finegold
Michelle & Jan Hagemeier
Chris Hogbin
Mark Kelly & Margaret
  McDonald Kelly
Nicola Kerr
Emma O'Donoghue
Tracy Phillips
Suzanne Pirret
Theo & Barbara Priovolos
Sir Paul & Lady Ruddock
Carol Sellars
Maria Sukkar
Jan & Michael Topham
Maureen & Tony Wheeler
Anonymous

Directors' Circle
Mrs Asli Arah
Ms Sophia Arnold
Dr Kate Best
Katie Bradford
Piers Butler
Sir Trevor & Lady Chinn
Joachim Fleury
David & Julie Frusher
Julian & Ana Garel-Jones
Louis Greig
David & Claudia Harding
Dr Timothy Hyde
Roderick & Elizabeth Jack
Mrs Joan Kingsley
Victoria Leggett
Emma Marsh
Rachel Mason
Andrew & Ariana Rodger
Simon Tuttle
Anonymous

Platinum Members
Simon A Aldridge
Moira Andreae
Nick Archdale
Anthony Burton CBE
Clive & Helena Butler
Gavin & Lesley Casey
Sarah & Philippe Chappatte
Andrea & Anthony Coombs
Clyde Cooper
Victoria Corcoran
Mrs Lara Cross
Andrew & Amanda Cryer
Shane & Catherine Cullinane
Matthew Dean
Sarah Denning
Caroline Diamond
Cherry & Rob Dickins
The Drabble Family
Denise & Randolph Dumas
Robyn Durie
Mark & Sarah Evans
Sally & Giles Everist
Celeste Fenichel
Emily Fletcher
The Edwin Fox Foundation
Dominic & Claire Freemantle
Beverley Gee
Nick & Julie Gould
The Richard Grand Foundation
Jill Hackel & Andrzej Zarzycki
Carol Hall
Sam & Caroline Haubold
Mr & Mrs Gordon Holmes
Soyar Hophinson
Damien Hyland
Amanda & Chris Jennings
Ralph Kanter
Jim & Wendy Karp
David P Kaskel
  & Christopher A Teano
Vincent & Amanda Keaveny
Peter & Maria Kellner
Mr & Mrs Pawel Kisielewski
Rosemary Leith
Mark & Sophie Lewisohn
Kathryn Ludlow
The Maplescombe Trust
Christopher Marek Rencki
Frederic Marguerre
Mrs Janet Martin
Andrew McIver
David & Elizabeth Miles
Jameson & Lauren Miller
Barbara Minto
M.E. Murphy Altschuler
Siobhan Murphy
Peter & Maggie Murray-Smith
Sarah Muscat
Liv Nilssen
Andrea & Hilary Ponti
Greg & Karen Reid
Nick & Annie Reid
Corinne Rooney
William & Hilary Russell

Sally & Anthony Salz
Anita Scott
Bhags Sharma
Dr. Wendy Sigle
Andy Simpkin
Paul & Rita Skinner
Brian Smith
John Soler & Meg Morrison
Kim Taylor-Smith
Mrs Caroline Thomas
The Ulrich Family
Monica B Voldstad
Arrelle & François Von Hurter
Mr N C Wiggins
Anne-Marie Williams
Sir Robert & Lady Wilson
Anonymous

With thanks to our Friends, Silver and Gold Members whose support we greatly appreciate.

DEVELOPMENT COUNCIL

Piers Butler
Chris Cabot
Cas Donald
Sally Everist
Celeste Fenichel
Virginia Finegold
Tim Hincks
Anatol Orient
Andrew Rodger
Sian Westerman

Our Supporters contribute to all aspects of the Royal Court's work including: productions, commissions, writers' groups, International, Participation and Young Court, creative posts, the Trainee scheme and access initiatives as well as providing in-kind support.

For more information or to become a Supporter please contact: support@royalcourttheatre.com/ 020 7565 5049.

ROYAL

BAR & KITCHEN

The Royal Court's Bar & Kitchen aims to create a welcoming and inspiring environment with a style and ethos that reflects the work we put on stage. Our menu consists of simple, ingredient driven and flavour-focused dishes with an emphasis on freshness and seasonality. This is supported by a carefully curated drinks list notable for its excellent wine selection, craft beers and skilfully prepared coffee. By day a perfect spot for long lunches, meetings or quiet reflection and by night an atmospheric, vibrant meeting space for cast, crew, audiences and the general public.

GENERAL OPENING HOURS
Monday – Friday: 10am – late
Saturday: 12noon – late

Advance booking is suggested at peak times.

For more information, visit
royalcourttheatre.com/bar

HIRES & EVENTS

The Royal Court is available to hire for celebrations, rehearsals, meetings, filming, ceremonies and much more. Our two theatre spaces can be hired for conferences and showcases, and the building is a unique venue for bespoke weddings and receptions.

For more information, visit
royalcourttheatre.com/events

Sloane Square London, SW1W 8AS ⊖ Sloane Square ⇌ Victoria Station
🐦 royalcourt f royalcourttheatre

COURT

"There are no spaces, no rooms in my opinion, with a greater legacy of fearlessness, truth and clarity than this space."

Simon Stephens, Associate Playwright

The Royal Court invests in the future of the theatre, offering writers the support, time and resources to find their voices and tell their stories, asking the big questions and responding to the issues of the moment.

As a registered charity, the Royal Court needs to raise at least £1.5 million every year in addition to our Arts Council funding and ticket income, to keep seeking out, developing and nurturing new voices. Please join us by donating today.

You can donate online at **royalcourttheatre.com/donate** or via our **donation box in the Bar & Kitchen.**

We can't do it without you.

Support the Court

To find out more about the different ways in which you can be involved please contact support@royalcourttheatre.com/ 020 7565 5049

The English Stage Company at the Royal Court Theatre is a registered charity (No. 231242).

SUPERHOE

Nicôle Lecky

'After darkness, there must always be light.'

Acknowledgements

Thank you to my agents Elinor Burns and Rachel Taylor at Casarotto, what a year it's been! You have both been a constant source of support, joy and guidance. To my agents Femi Oguns and Jonathan Hall at IAG, thank you for all the positive energy and for giving me time and space to work on this project.

Thank you to Hamish Pirie, Vicky Featherstone, Lucy Davies, Michael Buffong, and Jane Fallowfield for believing in this play and me! You put my debut play on the Royal Court stage, and for that I'll be eternally grateful and probably won't leave any of you alone. Thank you to all the people at Talawa, the Royal Court and beyond for making this play possible. Jade Lewis, who would have thought that less than a year after meeting up in that coffee shop, that we'd be here. Thank you for your directing magic, girllllll. Corin aka The Last Skeptik, you are a G. Thank you for the music and the chats.

This play is dedicated to my mum, who I think of always. Mum, thank you from the depths of my heart for believing in me, and encouraging me to feel like I could achieve anything.

Joanne, you truly are the best sister in the world. It is I, who loves you more. It is in print now, so it cannot be disputed.

To my family, thank you for always supporting me whether it be words of encouragement, travelling to watch my shows or just making me laugh lots.

To my adopted family. Osy, you championed me from day one, even when I couldn't see it myself. Your friendship is immeasurable. Zack, my brother, thank you for showing up always. In so many ways. Stella, your encouragement never fails to uplift me. You are a Queen. Jason, you go out of your way for me. Thank you for pushing me, and for having such belief in me. Kiell, thank you for your time and help, and for always being a dear friend to me.

To all the women I spoke to and who shared stories with me, thank you. Thank you for your honesty, passion and openness. Thank you for your courage, to be able to share your most intimate memories with me – good and bad. You are forever powerful.

Nicôle, let this be a reminder that you can, even when you think you can't. Thank God for the strength, and breathe deep always.

Characters

SASHA CLAYTON, *twenty-four, mixed race, East London accent, aggy*

All other key characters

LAURA CLAYTON/McBRIDE, *Mum, white, early forties*
KEVIN McBRIDE, *stepdad, white, forties*
MEGAN McBRIDE, *half-sister, white and blonde, fifteen*
CARLY VISIONZ, *escort friend, white, early twenties*
ANTON SPENCER, *boyfriend, Black Caribbean, late twenties*
DELROSE, *Anton's neighbour, Jamaican, late fifties*
ALI, *regular client, Middle-Eastern, forties*
SALEEM, *acquaintance, Somalian, twenties*
LUCY DAVIS, *old friend, white, twenties*

Note on Text

This is a play for a single performer.

This text went to press before the end of rehearsals and so may differ slightly from the play as performed.

Scene One

SASHA *enters the space. A microphone stand. She smiles and waves at the audience.*

Thanks for coming. I wanna let you all know that my EP is dropping after this Live Lounge. Thank you to my manager, and my label for supporting me. Thanks to my man Anton, for always being there. And lastly thank you to you guys, for showing me bare love.

SASHA *performs a track: 'Picture Perfect'.*

> Stay,
> I'm taking a selfie of us
> Look in to the camera, don't blush
> We are flawless, we are
>
> When we're old
> We'll be reminded of the good times
> When we're old
> We'll see how dope we looked together
>
> **Picture perfect under the stars we are**
> **Picture perfect, under the stars we are**

[*Suggested interruption by* SASHA*'s mum from page 6, or wherever feels appropriate.*]

> Stay, just like that
> I'm close to falling in love
> Over and over, again
> I'll never stop falling, I swear
>
> When we're old
> We'll be reminded of the good times
> When we're old
> We'll see how dope we looked together
>
> **Picture perfect under the stars we are**
> **Picture perfect, under the stars we are**

Offstage, SASHA*'s mum calls her.* SASHA *reacts to this.*

'WHAT?! FOR FUCK SAKE! WHAT DO YOU WANT?!'

Beat.

'I WAS RECORDING A SONG! YOU'VE FUCKING RUINED IT NOW!'

Beat.

'FUCK DO YOU KNOW? YES I WAS ACTUALLY!'

Beat. Turns off laptop/music. She picks up and lights a half-smoked spliff from an ashtray.

Even though it's not finished yet, I might send out a few tracks off my EP to a couple of music people. Maybe meet some artists that wanna collab on it, coz I'm not on doing any of that YouTube shi–

'NO I AM NOT SMOKING THANK YOU VERY MUCH!'

She's so – (*Mimics suffocating.*) I thought I'd have my own house by now – not putting up with these fuckers always moaning. Kevin – my stepdad, he's got all these bastard rules. If you're sat next to him texting he gets annoyed, and don't even think about watching anything good on the telly, like *Love Island* or Kardashians. 'Reality TV is for idiots which is made to detract us all from the real issues.'

I'm like 'What real issues?'

Kevin goes on a rant about real celebrities in his day, and how my generation is self-obsessed. 'If you're not careful, your generation will end up with rotting brains.'

'If I'm not careful? Am I responsible for my entire generation then? What's *Loose Women* if it's not a bunch of slags chatting bare shit?'

Beat.

'That's daytime telly, that's a bit different Sasha.' My mum pipes up.

These two wind me right up the fucking wall.

Beat. SASHA *drinks from a can of Red Stripe.*

I go downstairs, and they're all there stood round the fucking kitchen table, with loads of shopping bags. I lean on the doorframe trying to not make it bait that I'm high again, they don't look at me anyway.

Clears throat.

'Bought me anything?'

'Why would they buy YOU anything?'

This is Megan. Megan is my little sister and she's a bitch. Kevin gives Megan a squeeze on the shoulder, it's a 'don't let Sasha irritate you' squeeze.

'Well it's not your money so mind your business.'

'Well you're twenty-four you should buy things for yourself.'

'Well one: I haven't got any money so how am I supposed to buy things for myself, and two: Shut your fucking mouth how about that?'

'Hey hey hey Sasha. Less of that okay. Less of that.'

Beat. SASHA *picks up a bag.*

'Since when do we shop at Debenhams.'

'I've always gone to Debenhams.'

'You've always "window-shopped" at Debenhams. You don't GO to Debenhams Mum.'

SASHA *looks in the bag.*

'Sixty pound for a pair of pillowcases?'

'That's because you only shop in Primark.'

Megan chuckles and I wonder what she's gonna do when she actually turns sixteen. I think it's legal to beat up a sixteen-year-old, she's got about another seven months until I kick her in her cunt back to her dead dad's grave…

Beat.

Megan makes up shit about the time her dad took her to Kids Kingdom. I was thirteen when he died so I know that didn't happen. I do remember when he sold the TV that I had in my room, or the time he made me get out the car, and pick up drugs for him. My mum never had a problem with drugs back then, now she kicks off when she can smell even a hint of weed. My mum is born and bred in East London, and Kevin isn't like any of the men my mum used to date. She had me at seventeen, and she used to go from bad guy to bad guy, including my dad. Everything that happened pre-Kevin, has somehow been erased.

Beat.

We were broke as fuck before Kevin showed up. Megan got sent to a posh school, I never.

'Primark Princess to the rescue! The reason you don't have any money to buy your own things is because you don't have a job and you sit in your bedroom making "tracks". Even though you're too scared to post them online, because you know they won't get any likes.'

I fix Megan with a cold-as-fuck look, but Kevin steps in before it gets out of hand.

'Sasha my parents are over this evening for dinner, will you be around?'

Ah so this is why they called me downstairs.

SASHA *studies Kevin.*

I wouldn't be surprised if Kevin dyes his hair, it's a proper box-job grey. My mum and Megan go to the salon together. My mum tried to get me to go with 'em, and I told her they didn't cut hair like mine – maybe she should check next time rather than subjecting me to a woman who's never cut curly hair before.

Beat.

The two of them like this blonde mummy-and-daughter combo. The perfect trio and then there's me.

Beat.

I live in Plaistow. Plaistow/Stratford. I liked growing up round here, everyone was kinda on the same level you know. It's London, but we still played out. Knock Down Gingers, and run-outs by the blue-and-white maisonettes. The cars pulling in, and tryna dodge 'em to make it back to base. We used to push eggs through letterboxes when it was Halloween, we were a bunch of shits. But I had fun, it was just before kids started getting phones and using the internet. I grew up on chicken and chips. I was bred on that shit, and Fat Chaps when I could afford the chilli sauce. I walk through Stratford Rec, and think about when I used to pick daffodils for Mum on Mother's Day. All excited for her, that was when Megan and I got on, she was a really cute baby.

Shit! It's Lucy Davis. I've not seen her properly for about five years and it's definitely her. There's no way we're not gonna bump into one another. It's gonna be awkward, and we do bump into each other. And it's fucking awkward.

'You alright?'

Lucy says her and her boyfriend are briefly in town, and she talks about how much Stratford has changed, what with the huge Westfield and Olympic Park. Buying a house is impossible for her mum. All the hipsters have come in, pushing everyone out… I don't really know when she got this smart and confident. Talking about politics.

'Where are you living now?'

'I've bought! Limehouse. Still close to the endz to see Mum and Megan but cheaper than Stratford.'

Lucy used to be my bestest friend. She went away to uni, and then we didn't have anything in common any more. All the new friends she had looked like Ellie Goulding, and she started singing along to the Kaiser Chiefs and getting offended whenever I used the word retard. Suddenly I was too ghetto for her, and she became this stuck-up snob even though her mum's been chiefing the benefit system for time.

I carry on walking towards Bow, and my throat feels thick. My stomach feels all weird and I feel ill. I feel like I might be sick so I sit down at the bus stop, and think about how nice it will be to see Anton. Sometimes my body does that, or I feel like my

head might explode or I get really sweaty hands. I start to feel
really panicky, like a right weirdo. Once it lasted for two
months, but I just kept smoking weed until I felt alright again.

Beat.

I'm at Anton's house, and Delrose – Anton's next-door
neighbour – opens the door. She's round there a lot, watering
the plants or whatever else Anton's mum has got her doing.
Anton's mum is always in Jamaica. Even when Anton was little,
he'd come back to an empty house. She'd go away for weeks on
end and leave him bulk-buy boxes of cereal and pancake mix
from Costco. Delrose is Jamaican as well and she always says
bare wise shit. She's a teacher at a secondary school round the
corner. She's got a son but he's got issues, he's always
screaming even though he's like forty or something. Delrose
says a prayer and gets on with it.

'How is yuh music going?'

I tell her that my EP is gonna make waves. She tells me that
she's been visiting Dionn, Anton's brother in prison.

'He's doing alright. Been reading and whatnot, he's excited
about getting out.'

I nod before rushing past Delrose and into Anton's room. I don't
think Anton will mind me being here. I've not spoken to him for
a bit, he gets very very busy. Anton didn't used to do proper
work, he used to deal drugs a bit and do music and like odd
jobs. He was a proper businessman like Alan Sugar... I dropped
out of uni because you don't really need a degree to do music.
Plus everyone was bare annoying, and always wanting to go to
Nando's on these big group outings. I was like 'Nah you're
alright.' Anton wears a suit now and he's got all these new
mates and works-drink things.

Beat.

Anton is like... how I remember circling presents in the Argos
catalogue, just praying on Christmas Day you would get them.
Except, imagine circling just one toy because it's that amazing
and then you actually get it. He's got this beautiful face, the
smoothest skin you've ever touched and these really rough

kind of dry hands. And yet they're so soft at the same time. He's the only man I've ever loved. And I mean that, I've never loved another man, not even a family member. Anton is three years older than me, I was thirteen when we got together. He's taught me more than anyone, he taught me how to handle myself and not be mugged off. How to strap a zoot. He taught me pleasure, his tongue between my thighs is my favourite thing in the world.

Beat.

I can hear Delrose coming up the stairs, I lie down on Anton's bed and pretend to be asleep. I've done this before. She comes in the room, and calls my name a few times before shaking me gently.

'Stay on da right path and put yuhself first, even before Anton. Yah need to remember that men come and go but yuh stuck with yuhself forever.'

I find that an odd thing to say, why wouldn't I be with Anton forever? What does she even know about anything? She tries to hug me before I leave, but I shake her off – this bloody woman is always on job. I must have been there for longer than I realised, because it's darkest winter outside and it's cold. The wind stings my lips as I head home.

As I stand outside my front door, I pray that Anton calls me tonight or I don't know what I'll do. Before I go in I peer through the window, and see everyone round the table eating a roast dinner. Kevin's parents are there, and Megan's friend Martha is sitting on my seat, the little cunt. I feel like Harry Potter, when they shove him in that cupboard under the stairs. Except I'm not Harry Potter, I'm Voldemort, so I go in, and I make sure to slam the front door as I do.

The lights dim. In SASHA*'s bedroom.*

I'm in my room now shut up like bloody Quasimodo and I'm fucking Sasha Clayton. I've made a sick EP. I was the most popular girl in my school. Anton ain't rung me. He ain't rung me and I ain't spoke to him for two weeks. TWO weeks. What is going on? I swear I'm gonna let everyone know who the fucking hell I am!

She puts her hood up and raps.

Track: 'Anton'.

Alright 'ello

Kevin you're a gangly fucking prick
Mum you are a Top TOP snitch
Megan you're a scheming little bitch
And everybody else you can suck my clit

How's about I got a little story that I wanna tell you,
It goes fuck you, fuck you and yeah fuck you too, cah
You man are moving like dickheads, which I don't
    deserve
Treating me like I should be lying down, beneath the dirt

Anton can you please pick up the phone
Can you please pick up now, hello
Nah it's not even a joke
Answer the bludclart phone

So me and you been together nearly, what, eleven years
    now
You think you can ghost me? This is how this shit is
    playing out?
Nah until I say otherwise, you're my man always and
    forever
We are Jay and Beyoncé, we are staying together

Listen, I would like some respect
I don't want to have to ask for it again
I'd really like to not go insane
But you're a fuckboi and yeah, you're the one to the
    blame

Anton can you please pick up the phone
Can you please pick up now, hello
Nah it's not even a joke
Answer the bludclart phone

Skanks and then tries to call him.

I've left you twelve missed calls,
What d'yu think this is,

And you still ain't called me back...
Anton, are you taking the piss?

(*To audience member.*) Bet your man calls you back...

Kisses teeth.

The track fades out.

Scene Two

The next day I've blacked out again. I got too high. I google
how many units a week it takes to make you an alcoholic.

Beat. Checks phone.

I don't fucking need that this early in the morning. I go on my
Instagram and I see that I posted a quote last night. I can't even
look at it properly... I've got beads of sweat curled under my
baby hairs... I click on the image and it says I've posted it at 5
a.m. 'Fuck your memories, fuck fake feelings and fuck you' and
I've put a purple devil underneath. I've got eleven likes but I
quickly delete it. I don't know what the fuck that's about... I've
got the fear. I need to get a breakfast down me.

SASHA *checks the time.*

It's 3 p.m., fuck me how long have I slept? There's a kebab
wrapper near my bin, all of the yellow chips spilling out of it
like a strewn bouquet. Covered in blood red. I don't like it, it
makes me feel funny looking at it. I feel odd again. I always get
a bit weird when I can't quite remember...

I traipse downstairs into the kitchen, Kevin's wallet's on the
side and I borrow a tenner out of it.

'You alright Mum?'

She's off work because it's Saturday, and yet she looks like she
ain't slept a wink. I miss this you know, just being around her
without the other two. Not when she's mad at me, but we used

to have a lot of fun me and Mum. I wanna say, 'Can I get into your bed and cuddle up and watch *Lady and the Tramp* like we used to?'

A moment, SASHA *can't bring herself to ask for help.*

'You want a coffee?'

'No thanks Sasha, I drink tea.'

I should know that but I don't. Am I the prick here? I got some booky skunk off Ricardo and that can always go one way or the other.

'Why did you behave like that last night Sasha? You always show me up in front of Kevin's parents. What did you do with Kevin's mum's coat?'

Kevin's mum's coat? Fuck. I don't even remember seeing them.

'I don't know why you can't just be better – good even? Like…'

She wants to say Megan.

Silence.

'I'm going try more okay. Starting from now…

SASHA *puts on a fake-American accent.*

Because you are the winner of our Mom of the Year Prize! How about I make you a hamburger ma'am? With fries, and a chocolate milkshake?!'

I'm pulling food out the fridge and Mum is laughing. I haven't made her laugh in a while, the front door goes and I tell her to – 'Sit down.' Kevin's calling out my mum's name as he walks through the lounge and into the kitchen. He's stood there with two police officers. He looks unsure of how to proceed, but he definitely looks my way.

I tell myself to stay cool, this might be nothing to do with me. Maybe Megan's been beaten up or run over?…

'Sasha Clayton?'

Beat.

'Do you know Anton Spencer?' The fat policeman talks first. 'Where he lives? Were you round there yesterday?'

SASHA *doesn't say anything*.

'Did you hear the questions? Do you understand the questions?'

I look down at the table, my mum is panicking. 'Has something happened to Anton?'

It's the turn of the skinny policeman to talk.

'We're just here for an informal chat. Last night someone set fire to Anton Spencer's front garden. No one was injured luckily in the fire, but the people inside could have been trapped. You have a previous criminal conviction.'

Kevin's eyes do a one-eighty in his head – he didn't know about that. I wanna yell that it's only a conviction for fraud, but I say nothing. I don't like the skinny officer, I can tell he wanks to weird porn and probably eats Beef McCoy crisps. Megan's been listening on the stairs – and she comes in smiling.

'I woke up last night, I heard someone go out, the door slammed and I jumped. Was that you Sasha?'

My mum quickly tells the officers that it was her, to let the cat out, she looks at Kevin to verify it. He barely nods. He ain't about that life, he ain't going to prison for me.

'Right that's all we need for now. Someone will be back if they have any other questions, and I suggest you answer them when they do. Turning up uninvited to your ex-boyfriend's house, then hours later it's set on –

'I'm not Anton's "ex"-girlfriend!'

'It speaks. Well whatever you were.'

'I'm his girlfriend! Do you know if Anton's phone's working?'

The police look at one another and say their goodbyes. I wanna scream that it's my right to know what's happening! Megan looks like this is the biggest bit of tea she has ever seen spilt. My mum is really red now. She asks me what's going on with me and Anton?

'We're on a temporary hiatus, not that it's anyone's business.'

'No Anton dumped her because she's been cheating on him!'

I pull out my phone. I need to get some weed now.

'Are you listening Sasha – this is serious?'

'I can do two things at once Ke-vin.'

'You are irresponsible Sasha, you stay in your room all day and then stay out all night and you spent your grandma's money on this music thing. Without so much as thinking me and your mum might need a penny.'

'It's an as-yet-unreleased EP thank you. So I WILL be getting the money back. What do you lot need the money for? Loads of people stay at home now and they don't pay shit, they get an allowance. No one moves out any more, you should feel lucky I'm even here.'

'Sasha we're moving. We've been trying to tell you.'

'Moving where?'

'Away. From you, we need space to breathe.'

'Errr where am I going then?'

My mum looks like she wants to speak, but Kevin steps forward and puts his arm round her.

'I don't know Sasha, you'll have to get your own place. Every chance we've given you has been thrown back in our faces. That's the second time the police have shown up. Megan needs security and you are twenty-four now.'

I look at my mum and she's got tears in her eyes, I guess that's why she's been up all night. He sighs heavily, I can sense that this is my opportunity. I can feel my mum pleading with me to make it better.

Beat.

'You know what Kevin, you have the face of a nonce, so I'm not surprised you're always sticking up for Megan. You're probably trying to fuck her.'

The room is quiet. This doesn't go down well. I can tell by everyone's faces that I've gone too far this time.

Megan screams and lunges at me. All I know, is that I drag Megan down to the floor by her hair, my mum is frozen to the spot too scared to break it up. Kevin jumps in, and tries to pull me off and I turn around and shove him – hard in the nose. Then I threw up. I'm not sure why.

Scene Three

SASHA *on phone to the council.*

'I'm being kicked out of my house so I need somewhere to stay. I don't have a letter from my mum but I can easily get one, she doesn't want me here. Well what am I supposed to do if you lot won't help me? Do you want me to go out and sell my pussy on the street to get cash? You know what you are a fucking idiot I can tell – Hello! Hello?'

SASHA *kisses her teeth and hangs up.*

I'm fucked, I kinda thought they'd gimme a yard. I mean I ain't got nowhere to stay and they're asking me if I'm on the housing register and whether I've got kids and shit. Telling me it's best to try and work it out!

The other week my mum put a letter on my bed. Saying that before the sale is completed her and Kevin will help me find a place to rent. She can give me some money for a deposit but that she can't keep on giving. That I need to get a real job and learn how to be a self-sufficient adult.

SASHA *looks at her money jar.*

I'm not asking for shit. I have two hundred and seventy-one pounds and thirty-eight pence to my name...

Thinks.

Gonna ring Anton.

He doesn't answer.

I ring a few more people, seventeen to be exact until –

'Yo Saleem, how are you? Yeah it's Sasha, yeah from Docks. It's been a hot minute but I saw you last time at Ricardo's… Yeah a while back. This is gonna sound mad but I need somewhere to crash for a bit. If you got a room, I can pay you… Just a sofa. I don't mind – Is it? Okay okay. Well asap innit really. It'll be jokes okay. Tomorrow say no more. Aight G.'

SASHA *looks determined.*

Taking the piss! They proper thought I'd be crying begging to stay. I'll go to Saleem's keep my head down and work out my next move. Drop my EP.

Scene Four

The thing that annoyed me most when I got to Saleem's was that he's in a council flat. I'm running out of money, and everyone has a council flat except for me. I looked up places to rent and I can't afford shit plus 'I ain't got any credit' so I'm a bit fucked at the minute.

There's two bedrooms here but there's nothing in one of them so I'm sleeping in the living room. Something about Saleem makes me nervous. Sometimes I look at him when he doesn't realise and it's like he's talking to himself and he'll tap his head three times or randomly get up and spin. He tries to do it like he's forgotten something, but he has to spin to the left and the right and then he sits back down. Saleem keeps a Samurai sword on the wall in the living room. The last thing I see every night is that sword – keeping an eye on me he says.

Beat.

'I'm a singer-slash-rapper. I'm not the sort of girl that will be working in fucking Wetherspoons for eight pound an hour.'

'That's what I'm fucking talking about you dickhead. You're such an idiot, my mate works in a strip club and he can get you a job innit. You'll make bare P.'

'I ain't showing no one my pussy Saleem.'

'You showed me your fucking flaps just to sleep on my sofa, so why you acting prestige.'

'No I didn't.'

'Right so you banged me because you like me then issit?'

'I dunno, I just was... like... I don't know.'

Saleem starts pulling down his tracksuit bottoms.

'What are you doing?'

'You can suck my dick now then.'

I feel sick starting to rise in my throat, I move away from Saleem and my legs hit the back of the sofa.

'Fuck off Saleem.'

Silence.

He laughs and shakes his head. 'You're funny.' He leaves the room, I swear he's been tapping his head all day the fucking weirdo.

Beat.

I've been to strip clubs. Seen the women walking round with pint glasses begging for pound coins. I watched as this Eastern European girl span round a pole, she danced like she had an invisible elephant on her back. I could see the hairs on her skin standing up, and the pores on her bum cheek. Every time she bent over I had to look away. Anyway, I don't actually mind staying here for now, I've worked out how to handle Saleem. And he's right I do need to get a job.

SASHA *gets a text, checks her phone.*

'Hi love. It's Mum. You haven't replied yet? Could you please let me know where you're staying? Also, I had to give the police your number. Sorry!'

Fucking snitch talking to the police. I'm guessing it's about the fire that I ain't got fuck-all to do with. Maybe it's someone after Dionn, he did a lot of shit before he went inside. They don't think about him do they, only me number-one wrongun…

Pause.

There's always people in and out of Saleem's flat, people coming over to buy weed and whatever else Saleem has got his hands on. I usually sit in the empty room writing songs, that way I don't have to chat to all the crackheads. I'm in there one night when this girl walks in. She looks like she's stepped off a music video wearing a fur coat and jeans cut out at the sides and I can see she's not wearing any knickers.

'Are you Saleem's girlfriend?'

'No.'

'I was thinking what's a buff girl like you doing with him. He said that you might start stripping?'

SASHA *screws up her face.*

'What's it gotta do with you?'

'I know that stripping is dead rubbish now. I do stuff online, on social media, premium cam-work. You know what that is? You're like a virtual girlfriend that men can chat to and strip off for. My name's Carly.'

This Carly sounds like she's from up north, and it's very jarring to my ears.

'What's your name?'

'Sasha.'

'I thought you might be up for it Sasha?'

'I'm not.'

'We could make a lot of money together. You wanna sit in here your whole life getting high? Let me take your number for fuck sake, don't be so stoosh.'

SASHA *shrugs.*

'07913457654.'

'I'm serious we can make big money, ebony and ivory baby.'

She blows me a kiss and leaves. Ebony and ivory? Trying to take me for a dickhead. I'm not doing that I'm a singer, I'm gonna be famous so I can't have my fucking pussy out on the internet.

Beat. SASHA *has a drink. Thinks.*

I mean that girl looked like she had money. Kim Kardashian had a sex tape, she's the most famous woman in the world. Cardi B was a stripper, people love a rags-to-riches story. It's not like I'd have to actually touch these men, it's better than stripping.

Sasha gets a text from Carly, she reads it aloud.

'Call me, babycakes.'

That night I'm walking past the living room and I quickly run into the kitchen. I don't know if I'm seeing things but it looks like Saleem is in there tearing up the sofa with his Samurai sword... I hear the sound of leather ripping and the frame of the sofa banging against the wall.

'What if he comes in here with that sword?'

I should call Anton, because he's not gonna leave me to get my head sliced off by some mad yout! He hasn't blocked my number so obviously he still cares.

SASHA *decides to phone Anton. Thinks again. Places a call.*

Scene Five

Carly lives in Stepney Green and staying with Carly is kind of like when popcorn explodes in the microwave. You don't really know what she's gonna say or do next. She plans on being a millionaire by the time she's my age. I'm not saying I like Carly, I mean I don't trust no bitch so I'm not getting gassed but it feels like I'm on a permanent sleepover. And if Saleem had nothing in his flat, Carly is the opposite – it's like a page from the Littlewoods catalogue. She's honest about the fact that she gets botox and she had a fat transfer to make her ass bigger. She's got long straight hair down to her waist, it's shiny and silky like how I imagine a unicorn's tail to be. I get the feeling Carly did a lot of different shit before she came to London. She comes out with some random things.

'If your cousin's husband was a buff ting would you A) Bang him B) Suck him off or C) Cheeky snog?'

'Errr none of them, if that was my cousin's husband.'

'I'd pick C, and B... and A.'

She found it bare funny and I thought, fucking 'ell this must be northern banter. But then she goes, 'Man I miss Ian.'

SASHA *pulls a face*.

So she's obviously fucked her cousin's husband, but boi that's none of my business. Because she said I can stay here, and I plan to, until I can start making proper money. Carly said she'll spot me for rent and stuff, I said cool – well I ain't really got another option... She's taking a percentage off everything I earn too, this ain't out of the goodness of her heart. Listen Carly might think she's using me, making a little change off me and that but I got my head screwed on.

Track: 'Premium Pussy'.

> Bad bitch, slim waist
> Five-six, thick hips
> East London up in this bitch
>
> Let me give it to you straight
> Now I'm posting photos on a adult work page
> At first I was shy so you couldn't see my face
> Today I'm hitting angles see my lips see my waist
> Saying bye bye to the broke life, see ya
> Got a new name it's Sasha Alia
> Sleeping on the sofa living in fear
> Now I'm on the come-up, niggas I'm here
> There's thousands of girls just like me
> Open your Insta, what do you see

How do you think she got all that Gucci?
We're making racks, we're making P

I don't need a nine-to-five I just need a cam
Let them know with this premium pussy I can...
I don't need a day job, I don't need a man
Let them know with this premium pussy I can...
Premium pussy I can...

Buss it like a bad bitch, and I'm charging
Put the details of your card in
You can watch me on the cam,
Coz I've got a bigger plan
Take your money and I'm laughing

This is why you stay broke, you ain't tryna do the most
I'm making two bills a day from my phone
I decide what it's worth, first come first served
These guys just filling up my purse
You want monthly or just for the night?
Forty-five quid just to say hi
I'm in charge here I can set my price
First you get the fanbase then you monetise
Treat 'em like they're your friends, it's easy to pretend
You can rate their dick pics for a tens
I'll take a five-pound tip I'm not a snob
How's your day been? Tell me about your dog...

I don't need a nine-to-five I just need a cam
Let them know with this premium pussy I can...
I don't need a day job, I don't need a man
Let them know with this premium pussy I can...
Premium pussy I can...

Buss it like a bad bitch, and I'm charging
Put the details of your card in
You can watch me on the cam,
Coz I've got a bigger plan
Take your money and I'm laughing

Fifty per cent of the time, yeah I'm exposing myself
Rest of the time, yeah I'm promoting myself
It's an admin job, just like yours

But at least we workin for ourselves
You nine-to-fivers, you working for the man,
Living for the weekend, nothing in the bank
Wanna see my clit? Nah that's for the fans

Buss it like a bad bitch, and I'm charging
Put the details of your card in
You can watch me on the cam,
Coz I've got a bigger plan
Take your money and I'm laughing (*x2*)

Beat.

I have five PREMIUM followers, they're all white and defo
weird. But I'm playing the girlfriend card at the minute.

Thinks.

Yeah the black-girlfriend card, naughty black girl who needs
attention when black boyfriend is away. I'm learning people are
bare obsessed with calling me black, like get your black pussy
in my face, mine's kinda pink but I'm rolling with it. Carly's
got all these rules, I can't keep up. She likes that I'm getting
premium followers, but she wants more. So she put me up on
this website, and someone gifted me thirty pounds – coz I said I
wanted to buy a blender. These guys are fucking dumb. Talking
to me about their wives, and work and their erectile
dysfunction. It's kinda getting easy to encourage them to get
private access.

But the thing is when I think about it, I get kinda wet I'm not
gonna lie. Kinda sexy like posing and having people tell you
what nasty things they wanna do to you. Anton said I'm the
filthiest girl he's ever had sex with because I used to let him spit
in my mouth and choke me. Then he wouldn't talk to me the
next day.

Beat.

Carly knows everyone, so now her friends are kinda my mates.
She's friends with two girls from *Love Island* and they posted a
photo to their pages and I was in it and I got like six hundred
followers. I pray that Megan saw it, that dickhead. And because
of all the followers I'm getting, this DJ called DJ Spinner has

contacted me, to see if I can send him some music. He's a big deal, he DJs in all the London clubs and Marbella and he did it all official and sent me an email. Professional and that. And Carly introduced me to all these club promoters, and we get 'paid to party'. We dance around a table, get free drinks and at the end of the night they give us eighty pounds.

It's really weird when I think about the fact that only a few months ago I was living at home. Feels like time is going by really fast, one minute I was at my mum and Kevin's and now I'm doing cam-work. I've spoken to my mum a bit, but there's not really much to say. It's crazy how you can be so close to someone and then suddenly you're not. Anton, my mum, even Megan the little bitch, I miss cussing her.

Tonight we went to the sickest party you've ever been to in your whole life. I swear I've never had this many people watch my Insta story before! We get home, and Carly is racking up and she turns and kisses me. Proper. Not like when we kiss sometimes in the club, that's for jokes, but there's no one here to see. She's looking at me with these flirty eyes.

'Why don't we start doing videos together, you and me doing sexy stuff and having fun.'

'No thanks bruv.'

'It'll be jokes. Aren't you getting bored of all that solo wanking?'

'I don't actually wank properly on camera, I pretend.'

'I could make you cum for real Sasha!'

'I'm not a lesbian Carly fuck off.'

The thing about Carly's eyes is that they're hypnotising, they pierce through your soul.

'I know you've fucked girls before, we all have. All of us bad bitches anyway.'

I shake my head... she bends down and starts to kiss me so I close my eyes and think of Anton. I don't think I fancy Carly but I do miss being touched. I miss being wanted.

Scene Six

I'm in Kent fuck knows why, my mum is showing me around their new house. It's big. Very... family-looking. Except it's not my home, because I ain't even got the code to the wifi.

'I want you to see this Sasha...'

SASHA *shrugs*.

'Alright.'

I follow my mum into a bedroom, and she's opening it slowly like someone cutting an official ribbon. I go in and she asks me if I like it, but the walls are beige and there's nothing in there.

'What?'

Hang on. Is this supposed to be?

It's like I'm being offered a second, third, hundredth chance. I'm just starting to make proper cam money like I couldn't just stop, there's Carly and then I'd have to move to Kent. Although, it did look nice on the way up, I could focus on my EP again and I didn't ever plan on getting my fanny out. It's not something I planned for you know. Maybe I could get a job, learn to drive... Kevin walks in and rubs my mum's shoulder.

'Did you tell her then?'

My mum smiles.

'We're having a baby!'

SASHA *stares at the ground, she doesn't know what to say. Back on the defensive.*

'At your age?'

'I've been checked over Sasha, and when the baby is here, maybe you can come and stay with us in the spare room for a bit, when Kevin's mum's not here hmm?'

I'm seriously outnumbered in this family. That's four whites to one brown now. At dinner Megan's decided to join us, she sits at the table on her phone, she hasn't said a word to me until –

'How do YOU know Carly Visionz?'

SASHA *plays dumb*.

'Who?'

'Carly Visionz, she's like a famous Insta model and you're all over each other's pictures!'

'I live with her, she's my best friend, that's why.'

'That's not true.'

'It is Megan, Sasha's been telling us all about her music stuff, and her modelling. I can't tell you how proud I am.'

It's my mum, she starts crying? And Megan's eyes might pop out of her head. Kevin clears his throat.

'It's wonderful that we can all be here, every family has their ups and downs.

SASHA *watches Kevin, uncomfortable*.

'You have finally fought to make something of yourself. I'll leave you with this: "Whatever you think you deserve, is exactly what you will get."'

'I'm showing my cunt to people on the internet.'

I don't say that… Instead I rush my dinner and quickly leave, it's just Mum and me at the front door. She hugs me, but I don't hug her back, I go limp in her arms like one of my old dollies. She retreats, and pats me on the shoulder instead. I feel like an orphan.

I get the train back from Sevenoaks and I'm on my phone having my usual stalk, when a photo catches my eye. Anton's in the photo – smiling, he's got his arms around a girl and she's holding up a twenty-first birthday cake. The caption underneath says 'Happy birthday to me and happy one-year anniversary to my baby'. People I've never heard of calling them hashtag couplegoals. I try to blink back tears from my eyes, so I look outside the train carriage and see a woman begging on the platform. I feel, I dunno – like that could be me if I'm not careful.

SASHA *pauses, she's shared too much.* SASHA *looks back at the woman begging.*

Instead of going home, I realise I'm standing outside Anton's house. All the lights are off, he's probably still at the birthday party. I should wait for them to come back. And when they do I need to provoke her so that she hits me first. Then it's self-defence.

'Oh you like my sloppy seconds yeah? How do you feel knowing I used to sit on his – '

'Sasha!'

Damn! It's Delrose.

'What are you doing standing there in the dark? I don't think Anton's in, he might be out with Dionn. Him finally come out.'

Beat. SASHA *is frozen.*

'I don't care about Dionn!'

'Why don't you come round mine for a cup of tea?… Where are you living now? You disappeared! Perry asks after you… It's not easy out on your own, I mean it when I say you are always welcome round here. If you're lonely or – '

'I'm not lonely, I've got two thousand eight hundred followers. You're the one who's lonely living with your mentally deranged son.'

As soon as I say it I know I shouldn't have. But Delrose doesn't even flinch. She's got this look in her eyes, like a fuzzy ball of kindness mixed with pity. I turn away because I'm not gonna cry again.

'You've got my number Sasha, watch what yuh doin.'

When I get in, Carly's waiting for me.

'We are going out bitch. We are on the guestlist for Future's after-party!'

Carly jumps up and down shrieking and I have never been so glad to see her. In a weird way it's like Carly has become my family, she's the only one who really knows me now. This is the only thing that's real, making money and music so everyone else can go and fuck themselves.

Scene Seven

Carly's hooked up some easy-money work tonight, some hostessing thing. We basically put on a little dress, flirt with some old-ass men and drink champagne. When we get there it's at a Mayfair hotel on the top floor, and there are twenty other pretty-looking girls. The woman in charge looks like Lorraine Kelly, she tells us to have fun and gives us a glass of champagne to relax. There's one black man here and he's an ex-basketballer, it's his charity dinner to thank everyone for their donations. Over the night people hoover cocaine, and ask my opinion on bloody everything.

'Sasha, Sasha do you feel like your background has stopped you achieving things?'

They're arguing between themselves about the best way to 'disperse wealth'.

'Sasha when your grandparents came over what was the biggest challenge they faced?'

I shrug because I don't know.

When they finish eating, Carly announces that I want to sing a song. I freeze, praying the ground swallows me up, but the men start clapping. Cheering me on. I stand up. But I don't know nothing these old men will like, so I just sing 'More Than a Woman' by Aaliyah.

When I'm done one of the men hands me a rose off the table, and another picks me up and bends me backwards like I'm a superstar… I remember how much I love singing it's… I need it.

Track: 'Sing for Him'.

Fuck, I'm actually fucked.
I go to get some water.
The guy I'm sat next to follows me, he tells me to sing for him again – privately.

> He's telling me how impressed he is.
> Takes my hand as I let him lead me into a room
> I'm high off the singing plus I'm high.

I'm nervous as he stands and I watch his trousers rise
I've done a lot of coke…
He grabs my mouth hard and pushes me down
He is a pretty strong bloke
He shoves his fingers in my throat.
Trying his hardest to make me gag and choke
And it's all going so fast, rubbing his hands all over my ass.
As he takes my pants off
Pushing his fingers inside, tells me to say that I'm a
      whore.
And I think I might cry
I like it rough but this is really really fucking rough
He fucks and it's over
And I lay there raw
Why do I feel like I've been here before
I lay quiet, eyes on the door

He's telling me to sing for him,
Then he might fall, in love with me
He's telling me to sing for him
Oh oh oh (*x2*)

I'm intoxicated – I've never had sex on cocaine. Fuck.
      But I feel…
Shit and man Anton's right. I am filthy. I feel guilty.
Maybe there is something wrong with me?
Then the guy gets up and says 'The amount I'm paying,
the least you could have bothered to do – is wax it or
      shave it.'
And he slams the door, before I find my voice to say
'Who the fuck do you think you're talking to ey.'
But I'm naked so I can't run after him.
So I just stay there, in the bed, hyperventilating
I get up and walk into a room,
There's loads of people having sex and Carly's in there
      too
And I don't know what to do.
BREATHE. Hah, hah
I'm panicking.
Hah
I think that I might die

He's telling me to sing for him,
then he might fall, in love with me
He's telling me to sing for him
Oh oh oh (*x2*)

You're a pretty girl, but you're not a little girl any more. You're
a pretty girl, but you're not a little girl any more.

This is your brain talking. You ain't worth it, you deserved it,
you're useless, you ain't shit. You ain't shit Sasha. You ain't
shit.

> So spread your legs. Get on your knees. You could be the
> girl of his dreams.
> You could be the girl of his dreams, but you won't be
> Sasha. You won't be. Coz you ain't shit. Look at the
> life you're left with.
> You're lonely. Lonely lost little girl.
> And it hurts. No one to tell.
> Who would love you
> Who would like you. For you.
> Sasha Clayton, let me tell you from me to you.
> That you ain't shit. Ain't never been.
> You ain't shit Sasha.
> You ain't shit.

The next day.

I fall asleep on the sofa, and I wake up to Carly having a spliff
and some cash next to my phone.

'You ran off last night.'

'This money isn't for hostessing.'

Carly shrugs. She just shrugs!

'Don't take the piss Carly!'

Beat.

'You were fucking Saleem to stay on his sofa. So don't make
out like you got morals.'

Pause.

'Do you realise the room full of people that you were with last night? That could change both our lives, with money and connects. I thought you wanted to be a famous singer!'

'I do. But you pimped me out and you didn't even tell me! That guy was only having sex with me because he thought I was a fucking prostitute! He didn't actually like me!'

'So what! Most of the guys you've had sex with probably don't like you, they just wanna fuck. At least you're getting paid, cam-work was just the start. You can make big money. Trust me. If there were more women wanting to pay men for sex, men would be out selling their dicks in the street. They'd be proper gassed that they were so in demand, it's a fucking double standard and we're making the most of that. We've got all the power girl.'

There's a vice inside my brain squeezing so tight. Is Carly right? I don't know if it's because I don't feel like I have a lot of other options, or because I like the money. Maybe I like the attention. But the more money I'm getting does make me happier, you wouldn't understand if you've never been poor. I don't expect anyone to get it. So don't look at me like that.

Scene Eight

SASHA *semi-nude lying on a bed doing a webcam, whilst speaking the following.*

I live-stream on websites a lot now. It's easier to get a big hit of followers in one go and that way they already know they need to pay. This premium pussy is being put to work. This one guy likes me to film my fanny slapping against the camera, and I repeat his name 'Greg Greg Greg'. We text a lot, he probably pays the most out of anyone, his chat is fucking dry but I'm making two hundred pounds off him from all the vids he asks for. My whole social media is photos of me, me eating out in fancy restaurants, me on fake trips to Mexico and Paris. I look at my page sometimes and think 'Fuck me do I want her life,' then I realise I do have my life only it's slightly different.

Beat.

Since me and Carly had beef – we're cool now. Don't get it twisted I told her if she ever fucking lies to me again, I'll send her and her fake tits in a separate box back to Wigan.

Beat.

The next guy I slept with felt like a business deal. He was so nervous, and to be honest he didn't even wanna do anything at first. It made me feel so awkward, just sat there on the bed with him… I thought God I'll just get it over with.

Carly and I even joke about these guys… how we're the ones taking them for a ride. They're willing to pay, and we're willing to collect their money… more people would definitely get paid to fuck if they had the hustle that we've got. So I don't care what the haters think, or the people who write stupid comments online.

I'm meeting someone off of Instagram today for dinner – I haven't told Carly. Everything isn't her business and there's nothing wrong making a little something on the side, just for myself. The pupil becomes the master, you watch. Carly sticks it on me before I leave – I tell her I'm going to see a mate.

'I'm your only mate, where you going?'

I run out the door, and I meet him at a restaurant which has got this giant fish on the wall and everyone looks bare posh. My Loubs are clacking on the floor and I'm thinking you know what I ain't doing too bad for a girl from endz. Up in here with all these rich motherfuckers. The guy is called Ali, and he tells me he's about forty-odd and he's already waiting. Fuck me he's kinda hot, which surprises me because most of the men I've met aren't. He starts chatting bares straight away, asking me all these questions, how I got in to it and where I'm from originally and if business is going well and it's a bit much.

'How much are you fucking making asking me all these questions?'

He doesn't say anything but leans back and crosses his arms, and then he starts proper bussing up. And he points his finger at me saying 'Right right, okay okay, very true. Ask me a question.' He rests his hand on my forearm. I feel on the spot now, 'Why did you message me off Instagram and why are you paying someone for their... time?'

That's two questions he tells me, then he goes on to say that he stumbled across my page, and he didn't necessarily know that I was an escort until we got in to it. Some girls that look like me are, most aren't. He enjoys finding out.

'I didn't always do this.' It's like I want him to like me?

'Look, why should a beautiful girl give up her time for free, to a man who offers no commitment just sex and company? Only a poor man would argue that.'

He makes it sound noble. We eat and it feels like a proper date, I tell him about my music even though I haven't written anything in months. I haven't replied to that DJ yet, but I'm definitely going to. I'm busier now, with... this... the hustle has taken over. But once I'm sorted... Ali says he could see me being huge in America. Anton never took me anywhere, we used to sit in his room and smoke weed. Anyway, fuck Anton. When we finish dinner, we go outside and smoke. Ali has a taxi waiting for me, I'm confused. He kisses me on the cheek and tells the driver to take me home. He can sense that I'm not getting it. He hands me some cash, 'For the cab,' he says but it's far too much for a trip back to Stepney.

'I'll text you Sasha.'

He shuts the car door and I'm smiling. I hate that I like him, Carly said pretty early on do not like any of them or they'll fuck you over and she should know. You can't get into transactions with a man for sex and expect it to work out. But when I lie in bed that night I touch myself and I think of Ali. I cum and I feel like a top dickhead but I leave my phone on loud, just in case he rings.

Scene Nine

SASHA *drinks some wine and does a little cocaine.*

I'm trying to relax one evening, when Carly comes in storming like a tornado.

'You are gonna be thanking me when I tell ya this you bitch.'

SASHA *shrugs, as if to say 'Go on...'*

'We are going to Dubai! We are going to Dubai.'

Now I've never been that far on a plane, so at first I'm a bit nervous.

'I've got too much on.'

'Fuck you have, clear it. We're being paid to go and you ain't. seen. money. like. this. Think of the Instagram pics!'

'How much?'

'Three nights. Five grand nigga.'

'Carly!'

'Sorry not nigga, my bad. I'm excited! We're getting paid to go on holiday!'

'Yeah but what have we gotta do when we get there?'

'Alright so, the usual. Sex, and group sex. Sex with men and women.'

'So an orgy?... what else?'

'Anal.'

SASHA *lets out a huge groan.*

'What else?'

'They're paying not to wear condoms.'

'Nope. Bun that. Nah, nah nah. Why not?! They wanna pay five grand, to gives us bare diseases?!'

'Chill out Sash. We'll sort it, just palm them off on some of the other girls. We got each other's back yeah? It's gonna be proper jokes! Five grand my G!'

Carly grabs me and eventually we both start jumping around super-gassed, five grand is a lot of money. Dubai is going to be sick.

Beat.

The plane ride is wild. Carly gives me some diazepam to calm me down because I'm pranging out but it sends my head somewhere else. I fall asleep and I'm dreaming and there are spiders telling me to run away from this huge mouth that's trying to swallow me up, there's wind coming from the mouth and it's sucking me in. I manage to climb up the face and I realise it's Dionn's head... I wake up sweating as the plane lands with a thud.

Dubai is actually sick and we've got the first day to ourselves. Carly and I take photos on the beach and I can't – believe how nice it is, and how these photos look and I thank Carly coz my life has changed. She doesn't like mushy stuff, so we just spud and keep it moving so it's not gay.

In the night-time we go to a penthouse, we meet around fifteen men. There's a few other girls, so we start talking money – to make sure none of us are getting mugged off. There's a guy called Mo and he's in charge, he's fabulous but straight to the point. He tells me to say I'm half-Egyptian and white if anyone asks. I'm paired off with a man called Azzim and I hate his face. I keep texting Ali and Carly pulls me aside and tells me 'Not to fuck it up.'

One night we're at a huge mansion, somewhere by a beach and Carly comes running out of a room arguing with Mo about money and saying she was slapped... She tells me this man wants her to have sex with his son but he looks about thirteen. I tell her she should be happy that she didn't do it 'a slap is worth it, who cares if we get less money you can't fuck a kid!' She laughs:

'Happy I didn't do it?'

...She looks me dead in my eyes and it's the first time I think she actually might cry or scream – like from her gut. I've never been scared of Carly before, until I see her look like that...

Over the weekend, us girls have sex and touch each other whilst the guys half-look on and chat. It becomes a blur. I don't really clock who puts their hands on me or in me. The next day we leave and at the airport a girl called Amy cries. But instead of helping, we take a group pic of our passports. We're all in on it, even though we know it's fake. We hashtag 'Girls' Trip to Dubai'... I feel like a fraud but later that night I see Amy's social media. A photo of her on the beach, she looks like a goddess. The caption reads 'Best. Holiday. Ever.'

Scene Ten

Dubai feels like a dream, or a nightmare. It's hard to shake off but I try. Delrose keeps messaging me, I'm starting to think maybe Anton put her up to it but even I know that's a stupid thought. So I change my number. I've had that number since I was fourteen. It feels like I've lost something more than a phone number, that shit's like my identity. My serial number.

Beat.

I asked Ali if I could take a photo of the two of us but he said no. I said 'I could take one anyway while you're sleeping' and I laughed but I can tell he didn't find it funny. I told Ali that I'm not escorting for anyone else, only doing camera stuff and he shrugs.

Beat.

I can feel him slipping away since Dubai. Truth is we haven't had sex for three weeks, but he drops me home and I invite him in for the first time. Fuck what Carly thinks. To show him, you know, that it's different. Ali says he's got an early flight. He calls me pretty but I know he doesn't wanna see me again. I tell myself I'm wrong but I know I'm right. To be honest I don't even want to have sex with him, right now I don't care if I ever have sex again but I want him to hold me. He doesn't call me for ten days. I get drunk and I send him loads of proper aggy texts.

Pretends to text.

'Why haven't you called me? I know you're married and you can't have some non-Muslim brown girlfriend but you snort cocaine and you drink alcohol and yet I'm not good enough for you. You're a fucking joke mate. You are paying me for sex and you don't even wanna fuck me?'

I try to call him and the number doesn't connect. Carly can see I'm stressing out. I'm smoking every fifteen minutes and I'm always indoors now. She walks past me and says 'The hoe-wife never becomes the housewife babycakes.'

SASHA *looks out at the night, it's snowing.*

It's Christmas soon. I went and met Mum for a coffee. She said I should come and spend it with them. But all I could do was stare at her hand as she stroked her belly lovingly. She told me that Megan said to say hello, and that she wants to be a model just like me. I feel – I'm not ashamed. I'm not! Everyone lies online, I'm not the only one doing it. There's thousands of girls like me. I tell my mum I have plans for Christmas, and I do there's a Christmas Day rave on in central. My mum nods, but as she's leaving...

'I know I'm having this baby, but you'll always be my first you know that don't you. I was only a baby myself when I had you really, but I wouldn't change that for the world.'

SASHA *watches her mum go.*

That night I feel shaky again and I throw up like I used to do. Only this time, it's because I'm pregnant.

Beat.

It feels like I've aged a decade since meeting Carly. She sits with me in the back of the Uber on the way to the clinic, she tries to key a bit of coke out of a baggy.

'It's fucking 11 a.m. Carly.'

I knew it'd be a bad idea but she insisted on coming. That it's 'her job' as my employer to take me. That she takes all her girls to the clinic to do it.

'What girls?'

'What did you think you're the only girl working for me? No. It's just that you're the only saddo who needed somewhere to live. There's a lot you don't know about me Sasha.'

I try my hardest to tune her out. I think about the last time I was in a cab on my way to get an abortion, with Anton. We weren't ready and I was happy to be doing it. He made me feel like it was okay. Carly makes me feel worse. She tells me the fetus sends survival hormones to my brain trying to trick me into keeping it and that it knows what I'm planning. At the clinic the woman asks how many abortions I've had and I tell her it's my third... There was a time before Anton. I can't be sure but I think the woman rolls her eyes.

'What is there a limit on how many you can fucking have? No. So let me have the pill and I can go.'

That evening I sit on the toilet in agony whilst the baby that never was needles out of me. I'm not glad this time, I curl up into a ball and I cry.

Scene Eleven

Carly says there's been a curse on the house since Dubai, some boys have hacked her account. They keep sending her messages, saying that they're gonna expose her for being an escort. They've got a whole website, with photos of girls who say they're models but secretly do sex work. I scroll through it and breathe out hard because my page isn't on there – yet. I want my old life back and my old phone number and sitting in my old room smoking weed and making songs on my laptop. I look at photos of myself and I can't tell what's real any more, was I actually happy in that photo or was I pretending to be?

I'm fed up of being told what to do by Carly. She tries to get me out to a party tonight and I don't wanna go.

Beat.

Because I finally did it… I emailed that DJ back and I've arranged to meet him – in an hour. I sent him what I had from my EP, and he wants to meet. I felt like after what's happened, maybe I didn't have much to lose? And he likes it… But Carly is hassling me like crazy asking me what time I'll be back and I switch.

'I ain't fucking going Carly, I've got a meeting for my music, that's what I wanna be doing.'

'Music? Get off Sasha! I've known you how long, you haven't posted one song. You put up links of yourself getting naked, that's what you do. And that's what people like.'

'Maybe I can do other things.'

'I gave you two weeks to get over that abortion and now you wanna fuck off and waste time on that shit? You can't stay living here, if you're not gonna do what I fucking say. You do work for me, remember that much you ungrateful bitch.'

I can feel myself clenching my fists.

'What you gonna do Sasha you gonna fight me are yer? Are you really mad are yer? I don't fucking care. I'm sorry babycakes you're not unique, you're not the only buff girl on social media selling her pussy.'

My fists are still clenched, and the anger is seeping out of my body.

'Nah this is not me Carly. You knew what you were doing when you met me. You're a pimp! You've never been a friend to me, you've made me make the worst decisions I've ever made in my fucking life.'

'Don't kid on. You forget what you've told me? You were a fucking slag from long time before you met me, and we both know that.'

Silence. SASHA *stares at Carly.*

'You're not all bad like me Sasha, but you're bad enough.'

Track: 'Superhero'.

SASHA *casually takes a sip of water, looks out at the audience. Speaks to them directly. She laughs.*

I know I'm not performing. I know you're not really here. But I don't care, because I like the company, even if you're all made up...

I'm a superhero trying to find my way back home.
Going round in circles until the time that day comes
It comes
Ohhh the day it comes
I can stand on my own two feet, I just realised I don't
    need nobody to help me sleep, nobody to hold me
    tight.
I've got myself
I said I've got my fucking self.
I'm my own superhero

Yeah it's nice to have family and stuff,
It's nice to feel like you don't need to give up
Got anxiety playing on my mind
I got feelings all the time and I don't know what to do
    with 'em
Because they just move through my soul and then I feel
    like I'm losing control
It's okay to lose control
Baby girl
You're a superhero
I'm a superhero tryna find my way back home
Going round in circles until the time that day comes
It comes
I'm a superhero.

I thought I was lost
It doesn't matter what I've done
I can keep getting up, I can count to ten,
I can take a breath
I can finally exhale
And feel

I can FEEL
I'm gonna be okay
It doesn't matter what I did
Coz it's a new day today
I'm a superhero tryna find my way back home
Going round in circles until the time that day comes
I will find my way
My way at the end of the day
What I choose to do with my life is up to me
We're all superheroes
Tap in to your power
Tap in to your power.

I meet DJ Spinner in a bar in Dalston and he's very friendly. Bare enthusiastic, talking about how much he likes my page and all these record A-and-R guys that he knows, asking me what other music I'm working on.

'What would you say your sound is?'

I like singing, but I kinda like rap. I guess my sound is, my sound is... I don't know any more. I don't know, because I don't know who I am. But he's smiling, and I think he looks impressed. He tells me how much he loved my song 'Superhoe' and I freeze.

'My song called what?'

'Superhoe.'

'Did you listen to it?'

'Yeah, I... Boi I listened to the others, that's the name of the EP nah?'

'Are you just here to try and fuck me?'

'Business and pleasure is business and pleasure babes. I don't see why the two can't mix?'

The room starts to spin and my head gets hot. I'm going home. I don't even know what that means but I'm going home. I run out of the bar – I've gotta get out of there. I'm running. I am running for my life. Past people and shops and buses and spit on the floor and London life and people not giving a fuck that I feel

like I might really die this time. Die of heartbreak and
loneliness. I jump on a bus and I take it all the way to Anton's
house, I'm shivering when I get there, it's winter and I feel the
coldest I've ever felt. I stand outside staring at it, staring past
the burnt-out front garden that has been paved over. I spent
twelve years here. There are no lights on, then I see it the 'For
Sale' sign with the words 'Sold' stamped across it. A car pulls
up and I jump as the lights shine on me. It's Delrose.

'Sasha yuh look good! What yuh doing here?'

'Where've they gone? Delrose?!'

'What do you mean, they sold it?'

'Where did they go?'

'They moved because Dionn come out of prison, they didn't
want him living round here any more. Too much spilt milk.'

I'm shaking and I'm sick at the sound of Dionn's name.

'Come on Sasha let's get yuh inside.'

Delrose puts her arms around me, this is it. I've finally broken
and I always knew I would. She asks what happened with me
and Anton. I tell Delrose that before I met Anton I knew Dionn,
I used to hang around with him and his friends, smoking weed
and I used to have sex with them. I didn't really want to but
I had nowhere else to bunk off school. When Dionn went to
prison I never told Anton that I knew his brother because I really
liked him, he was kind to me and then we were together so long
I couldn't ever tell him. But I always regretted it. I swear. And
then suddenly people kept saying there was this video of me but
I don't remember! I don't even know if Anton saw it.

Delrose doesn't understand. She doesn't understand because I
would have only been about twelve if it was before Dionn went
to prison? Dionn and his friends would have been twenty-odd.
Delrose looks shaken, but places a hand on my head as tears fall
silently from my eyes.

'I've always been a mess, I always knew I'd have a fucked-up
life and that nothing good would ever happen. I ruin everything
for everyone.'

Delrose holds me and tells me I was too young to give consent and that everything will be okay because it wasn't my fault. That she will help me make this right, and that I can't keep blaming myself for what those boys convinced me to do. I don't need to be angry any more.

I fall into a sleep like I haven't slept for a thousand years and when I wake up Delrose is sat there with a cup of tea and a smile. She tells me that I've got to learn to forgive myself and that we must embrace the things that have happened to us – good or bad.

This afternoon I took my things from Carly's flat and moved them into Delrose's spare room. I thought Carly would try to stop me, but she just sat there on the floor in the hallway. I had to step over her when I finally left, and I felt sad, I actually felt sad for her because she looked really small – like someone's daughter. Waiting to be collected from school.

I'm only next door to that old house. Full of memories I've buried deep inside me but I feel like I'm a whole world away. A world away from Sasha Alia.

SASHA *gets a text from her mum. She acknowledges it.*

My mum.

SASHA *reads the text.*

The baby's started kicking. The police have sent a letter, saying there's no further action for the fire at Anton's house. 'A fresh start for you Sasha.'

Pause.

There's a knot in my stomach, a gnawing feeling I can't get rid of but it aches less than before. A lot less. Coz I don't think I deserve a second chance, but I feel like I've got new songs to write. Maybe that's enough for now.

The End.

A Nick Hern Book

Superhoe published as a paperback original in Great Britain in 2019 by Nick Hern Books Limited, The Glasshouse, 49a Goldhawk Road, London W12 8QP, in association with the Royal Court Theatre, London

Cover photography: Niall McDiarmid

Designed and typeset by Nick Hern Books, London
Printed in Great Britain by Mimeo Ltd, Huntingdon, Cambridgeshire PE29 6XX

A CIP catalogue record for this book is available from the British Library

ISBN   978 1 84842 838 6